Douglas G Abbott

Dedication

This book is dedicated to my late wife, Patricia A. Abbott and our late son, Keith D. Abbott. They rarely stopped smiling and made my life rich, rewarding and fun. They were always there when I needed them the most.

Table of Contents

Authors Biography - Douglas G Abbott

I was born August 16, 1938, at Paterson General Hospital to Florence Mills Abbott and Stuart Abbott. I was the third child of what would become a family of five children.

After living for two years in a rented home on Marion Street in the Totowa section of Paterson my family moved to a newly built home in the developing neighborhood on Emerson Avenue in the Hillcrest section. It would be the family home for the next twenty-one years.

My Mothers sister Alice Mills Skelton and her brother George N Mills and their families also bought homes on Emerson Avenue around the same time. Eventually I would have two Aunts, two Uncles, my maternal Grandmother and four cousins all living in a two-hundred-foot radius of my house. Obviously, we were a very close family which in the forties and fifties was the rule rather than the exception in Paterson.

After turning five years of age in 1943 I started Kindergarten at Public School #5 on Totowa Avenue. Eight- and one-half years later I graduated and started High School at Paterson Technical & Vocational HS. Contrary to perceptions at the time School #5 and Paterson Tech were both very good schools. They both had very dedicated teachers that provided me with an exceptional educational foundation. That training has served me very well for the sixty-seven years since my high school graduation.

On February 2, 1956, five days after my high school graduation, I along with six classmates joined the US Navy. We were very fortunate to be going into the service then. We were too young for the Korean War and Vietnam was still years away.

My time in the Navy was a three-and-a-half-year experience that included Aviation Preparatory School at NATTU Norman, OK, Aerographers Mate "A" and "C" schools at NAS/NTTU Lakehurst, NJ. Aerographers Mates are the Navy's Meteorologists.

After six months of schooling, I was assigned to the Staff of Commander – Amphibious Group Four. During this time, I got to help plan and execute mock amphibious landings in Panama, Sardinia and North Carolina.

After eighteen months in the staff assignment, I was transferred to the Destroyer Leader, USS Norfolk DL-1. This was primarily an antiaircraft and anti-submarine Ship. We operated in the Caribbean, Atlantic and North Atlantic doing anti-submarine operations. In early 1959 we received the first ASROC Anti-

Submarine Rocket fired torpedo system. The initial testing took place off Southern California at the Navy Test Facility on San Clemente Islandin the spring and summer of 1956,we were home ported in Long Beach, CA. In August of 1959 I was honorably discharged from the Navy and in September started college at Fairleigh Dickinson University in Teaneck, NJ. Initially majoring in Chemistry and Biology. I also began a career long association with the chemical industry by working as a part time lab technician while at Fairleigh Dickinson.

After two years in the laboratory as a technician and Tech Service Representative I became a full time Sales Representative in the Adhesive Resins Division of Morningstar-Paisley, Inc. Subsequent positions with Celanese Fibers Marketing Company and Celanese Specialty Resins as Regional Manager, National Sales Manager, and Distributor Manager led to my final position as Director- Corporate Accounts at the Shell Chemical Company where I retired.

The Shell Chemical Company was the fifth owner of Celanese Specialty Resins, the business that I joined in early 1982. I was incredibly lucky to survive all these transition processes that can be very challenging.

Currently I am enjoying my twentieth year of retirement living in Foley on the Gulf Coast of Alabama. My good fortune continues here as I am now in a wonderful relationship with Kathleen Marshall Kazanjian who I first met in 1958 when she was a waitress at Linwal's Restaurant on Rt 46 in Wayne, NJ. After failing to build a long-term relationship during our time together in 1958/1959 I finally "got the girl" from Packanack Lake 62 years later!

Naval Amphibious Base – Little Creek, VA

NAS Lakehurst, New Jersey

Paterson Technical & Vocational High School - Paterson, NJ

Paterson Technical & Vocational High School

SCHOOL NO. 5 PATERSON

Introduction

T hose of us who grew up in the forties and fifties are among the luckiest people who have ever lived. We were too young to either serve, or appreciate the sacrifices associated with WWII. Most of us were too young to serve in the Korean conflict and the majority managed to avoid the Vietnam war as well.

We started school in the early forties and the fifties at a time when the United States was clearly on the road to victory. The WWII era economy was robust to the point where unemployment was virtually nonexistent. For those not in the military the war years provided wages and salaries at levels never seen before. Domestically the largest concerns were over the rationing of food and gasoline.

The last half of the forties was a time of huge disruption of the economy and the requisite adjustments required to house, feed, and employ thousands of returning veterans.

By 1950 the disruption and adjustments were essentially complete resulting in a greatly expanded national economy that led to a decade of peace and prosperity that is unmatched in the history of the city, state and country.

On the downside the city's largest employer, the Wright Aeronautical Company, which was severely downsized after the war relocated it's still massive operations to Wood ridge in Bergen County. Simultaneously the large Textile industry accelerated its decline that began in the forties. By 1960 it was only a shadow of what it once was.

One small bench mark of this trend was the elimination of the Textile course at Paterson Technical & Vocational High School. Initshey day this program had two full time teachers and a large, well-equipped shop. By 1953 there were no students interested in majoring in the textile trades and the program was forced to disband.

By the 1960's Paterson's vibrant downtown retail stores were beginning to experience their own disruption. By the 1960's Paterson's vibrant down town retail stores were beginning to experience their own disruption. The suburban malls in Wayne and Paramus would provide very serious and often fatal competition for every segment of the retail market in Paterson.

Paterson – The City History

Paterson is the largest city in and the county seat of Passaic County, New Jersey. In the 2020 Census Paterson had a population of 159,732 making it the state's third most populous municipality.

The city was initially inhabited by the Algonquian speaking Native American Acquackanonk tribe of the Lenape also known as the Delaware Indians. The land was known as Lenapeho king. Originally claimed by the Dutch and called New Netherlands, it subsequently fell under British rule as the Province of New Jersey.

In this book we will concentrate on the period starting in 1940 when the population was 139,656 to 1960 where the city had grown to 143,663.

In 1791 Alexander Hamilton, the first US Secretary of the Treasury was instrumental in creating The Society for Useful Manufactures. This organization later became known as the S.U.M, or just the SUM. The SUM was Instrumental in the harvesting of energy from the Great Falls of the Passaic River. The primary purpose of these efforts by Hamilton and the SUM was to secure economic independence from British manufacturers. The Society subsequently founded the City of Paterson which became the cradle of the Industrial Revolution in America. Paterson is named for William Paterson, statesman, signer of the constitution and Governor of New Jersey who signed the 1782 Charter establishing the City of Paterson.

Pierre L'Enfant was an architect, engineer and city planner who had developed the initial plans for Washington, DC. He was also the initial planner for the SUM project. His proposed plan was to harness the power of The Great Falls through a rock channel and an aqueduct. The SUM's Director's felt that his plan was taking too long to complete, and he was over budget. He was replaced by Peter Colt in 1794 who then implemented a less complicated reservoir system to deliver the waterpower to the mills. Eventually problems developed with Colt's system and a design resembling L'Enfant's original plan was used after 1846.

The 77 foot high Great Falls along with a system of water raceways that harnessed the falls power provided energy for the mills downstream until 1914 when the SUM began generating hydroelectric power at the falls. The city experienced significant growth during this period. The SUM District originally included dozens of mill buildings and other manufacturing facilities associated with the textile Industry. Simultaneously the city was home to the manufacturers of firearms and railroad locomotives. In the latter half of the 19th century silk production of broad goods and narrow fabrics became the dominant industry and formed the basis of Paterson's most prosperous period, earning it the nickname "Silk City".

Hamilton's vision was to create an urban center that channeled the power of The Great Falls into an industrial powerhouse that turned Paterson into the nation's first planned industrial city. Over the years Paterson became a major center for industrial firsts:

- The first water powered cotton spinning mill (1793)
- The first continuous rolled paper (1812)
- The Colt Revolver (1836)
- The Rogers Locomotive Works which helped to fuel western expansion through the transcontinental railroad (1837)
- The Holland Submarine – Making underwater navigation possible (1878)

The Passaic Falls at Paterson, NJ – "The Great Falls"

One of Paterson's most famous industries was the Patent Arms Manufacturing Company, begun by Samuel Colt. In 1836, the Colt Gun Mill, a magnificent four-story brownstone building, was built on an area directly below the waterfalls. Here, Colt first manufactured his newly patented repeating firearm, the revolver, with mother of pearl handles, which were essential in securing the American frontier. Between 1836 and 1841, approximately 5,000 muskets rifles, and revolvers were made here.
Colt produced firearms here until 1842, when the company failed.

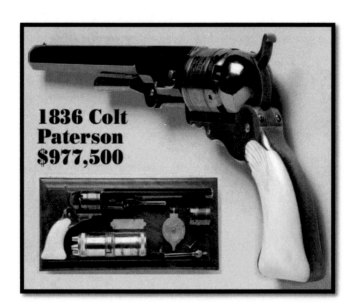

1836 Colt Paterson $977,500

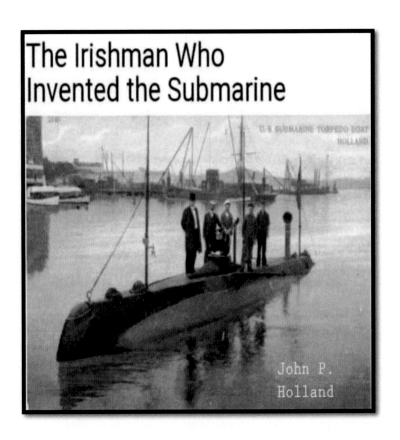

The Irishman Who Invented the Submarine

John P. Holland

John P Holland
Father of
Modern
Submarines

The Finian Ram pictured here is shown being moved from Westside Park toits current home at The Paterson Museum.

In the 1940 to 1960 period, we are focusing on in this book it is interesting to note that the SUM was still operating as a generator and reseller of electric power to many of Paterson's mills. My family's ribbon mill, Abbott Brothers was an SUM customer from 1906 until it ceased operation in 1960.

In 1835 Samuel Colt began producing firearms in Paterson, but within a few yearsthe business failed. In later years the family reorganized and relocated the business to Hartford, Connecticut.

Later in the 19th century Paterson was the site of early experiments and the development of submarines. An Irish/American school teacher and inventor, John Philip Holland is the acknowledged father of the modern submarines that are so critical to the countries defense. Two of Holland's early models sank during trials in the Passaic River. They were later recovered and are currently on display at the Paterson Museum located in the former Rogers Locomotive and Machine Works below the Falls at Market & Spruce streets. The larger boat recovered is the "Fenian Ram" The US Navy's first submarine is a direct descendant of the Fenian Ram that is in the Paterson Museum. After several iterations the USS Holland SS-1 was privately built and accepted by the Navy in 1898 and commissioned in 1900.

As a prominent mill town within the New York Metropolitan area Paterson has historically been known as the Silk City for its once pre-eminent role in silk manufacturing during the latter half of the nineteenth century and the first half of the twentieth century. Several significant related industries were concurrently established to service and support silk manufacturers. Among them were dyeing and finishing, textile printing, and the manufacture of a wide range of machinery to support the processing of raw silk, yarn creation, warp winding, weaving, dyeing & finishing and fabric printing. Along with the broad goods weaving of silk there were numerous companies weaving silk narrow fabrics & ribbon, jacquard labels & upholstery fabrics, jute weaving of burlap fabrics and Jute carpet backing as well as linen & silk thread.

Along with Newark and New York the brewing industry was booming in Paterson in the late 1800's. The Braun Brewery, Sprattler & Mennel, Graham Brewery, The Katz Brothers, and Burton Brewery merged in 1890 to form the Paterson Consolidated Brewing Company. In addition, the Hinchcliffe Brewing and Malting Company, founded in 1861, produced 75,000 barrels a year from its state-of-the-art facility at 63 Governor Street. Prohibition began in 1920 and lasted until 1933causing the demise of all the Paterson breweries.

Historically the city has been a mecca for immigrant laborers, particularly Italian weavers from the Naples region who came to work in the mills.

In 1913 Paterson's silk industry experienced the first of two large watershed events when years long labor unrest came to a head with the start of a prolonged strike that involved over

10,000 mill workers. The Paterson strikers organized after years of declining wages, continued poor working conditions, and long workdays. A secondary issue was the increasingly large number of women and children in the labor supply pool due to changing social customs that provided cheaper labor for the mill owners and reduced demand for more expensive male workers.

During this period the Paterson mills were dealing with intense competition from New England and Pennsylvania mills who were early adopters of new technology. During the strike many Paterson mills began to implement new, more efficient technology. High skill weavers, such as those in ribbon shops led the fight against multiple loom systems. The reduced labor intensity resulting from advanced technology also meant that many low skilled broad silk weavers would be displaced. However, all weavers were united in their efforts to shorten their work days and establish a minimum wage.

The strike began in February of 1913, and ended in failure five months later, on July 28. During the strike, approximately 1,850 strikers were arrested, including Industrial Workers of World (IWW) leaders Bill Haywood and Elizabeth Gurley Flynn.

At the time none of the primary demands were met. While unsuccessful at the time, the strike helped to forge the beginnings of what would become the modern labor movement, culminating in the end of child labor practices, decent working conditions for all workers and, ultimately the eight-hour day with the forty-hour work week.

The workforce, the mill owners and the city all suffered monumental losses because of the strike. At this time a gradual move by mill owners to lower cost areas such as Pennsylvania and the south began. By 1960 the entire Textile industry in Paterson would be close to nonexistence due in large part to high labor costs, regulatory issues, and tax burdens at the local, state& federal level.

Poster for the Paterson Silk Workers Strike Pageant at Madison Square Garden. Over 800 workers participated in the Strike Pageant that drew over 150,000 attendees.

IWW Leader Bill Haywood and his entourage in Paterson during the strike

Paterson Silk Strike Leaders

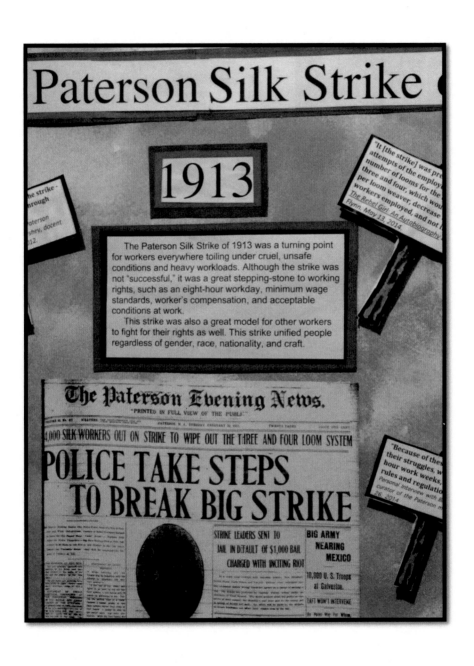

Paterson Silk Strike

1913

The Paterson Silk Strike of 1913 was a turning point for workers everywhere toiling under cruel, unsafe conditions and heavy workloads. Although the strike was not "successful," it was a great stepping-stone to working rights, such as an eight-hour workday, minimum wage standards, worker's compensation, and acceptable conditions at work.

This strike was also a great model for other workers to fight for their rights as well. This strike unified people regardless of gender, race, nationality, and craft.

The Paterson Evening News.
"PRINTED IN FULL VIEW OF THE PUBLIC"

...000 SILK WORKERS OUT ON STRIKE TO WIPE OUT THE THREE AND FOUR LOOM SYSTEM

POLICE TAKE STEPS TO BREAK BIG STRIKE

STRIKE LEADERS SENT TO JAIL IN DEFAULT OF $1,000 BAIL CHARGED WITH INCITING RIOT

BIG ARMY NEARING MEXICO

10,000 U. S. Troops at Galveston.

TAFT WON'T INTERVENE

Female and child labor in the silk mills

Paterson, N.J. Sept 21st 1900 - T&P #265 @ Rogers Locomotive Works
This was the method of transporting new locomotives from the Rogers Works to the Erie tracks - about 1 mile. 32 horses were used and this was the last locomotive hauled in them. After this a dummy engine was employed until the works were abandoned in 1926. The building on the left is the Paterson

THE ROSEN MILL
MARKET AND SPRUCE STREETS, PATERSON, N. J.

This Paterson mill site once housed the Union Works cotton factory and later
would be the base of Jacob Rosen & Sons. Founded by a Polish immigrant,
Jacob Rosen & Sons became a leading American manufacturer of silk ribbon,
with over a hundred looms in this building.

Paterson in WWII

I was a young kid attending school at PS 5 starting in September of 1943. Through the lens of a five-year-old my memory of Paterson and the war on the home front during this period is still reasonably clear. "Wrights", the Wright Aeronautical Company was clearly the dominant employer at this time. Everyone had either an immediate family member, or a relative that worked for "Wrights".

Much later in life I was able to learn just how important this company was, not only to Paterson, but to the country and the war effort as well.

What I did not know at the time was how big a strategic target the city was for potential air attacks. The Wright Aeronautical Company was one of two major producers of aircraft engines and propellers in the country. Huge numbers of fighters and bombers were equipped with Wrights famous "Whirlwind" brand of engines.

The city was home to several Anti-Air craft facilities. Every day going to and from School 5 I had to pass the Totowa Oval which was not the recreational facility that we know today.

During the war it was a serious Army Anti-Aircraft Base with two barracks of soldiers, large anti-aircraft guns and huge searchlights to spot and illuminate potential targets. After the war these large lights would be repurposed and show up at movie previews and store openings. It was a very impressive facility even to a kid of five to seven years of age.

My other memories of the war years included Air Raid Warning Sirens, Air raid drills and civilian Air Raid Wardens which my dad was one of. There were regular drives in school to sell War Bonds and collect Scrap metal for the war effort. Gasoline rationing was very strict with all vehicles displaying a windshield sticker that the quantity that the owner could purchase in a specified period. Foods such as Sugar, Butter and Meats were also strictly rationed. Families were often forced to do without until the new Ration Quota came into effect. A large percentage of families established and maintained "Victory Gardens" in their yards to supplement the foods subject to Rationing.

Plant No. 1 of Wright Aeronautical Corporation in Paterson, New Jersey

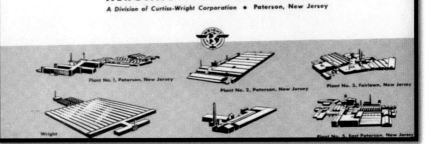

1943 near Main and Market Street, Paterson, New Jersey

A Parade to promote the sale of War Bonds

In the summer of 1945, my family was able to spend a couple of weeks in a rented house in Seaside Park, NJ. It was in early August, and I remember one of our family friends being on the beach with a very early model portable radio. It was a huge device that had to weigh at least forty pounds. For days it was always tuned in to an all-news station. Germany had surrendered earlier in the year and now everyone was waiting for the Japanese surrender that would finally end WWII. We had dropped Atomic Bombs earlier in the month with devastating effects in Japan.

Finally, the news came through that Japan was surrendering. Once the news began to spread, I witnessed the largest and most significant celebration of my young life.

The towns of Seaside Park and Seaside Heights were in absolute chaos for more than a day. In terms of "watershed" events in my life this one is either number one, or very close to it.

In Paterson the start of the war had a very large and immediate effect on the city's other major industry, the silk mills. Virtually all the silk in the world is produced by Japan and China. Clearly December 7, 1941, had the immediate effect of shutting off Silk Industries' only source of raw material.

After Pearl Harbor there was a very brief period before the government placed an embargo on all raw silk and silk yarn. It was critically needed for the manufacture of Parachutes for the military. At the time my family was in the Ribbon Weaving business using silk as its primary raw material. Once the government purchased all the existing silk inventories there was no choice but to find an alternative. The substitute material was Rayon, a synthetic fiber produced from Cellulose. Fortunately, there were three large, established American manufacturers in place producing Rayon yarn and the Paterson Silk industry was able to successfully make a rapid transition to the new material.

Post War Paterson

T he end of the war brought numerous and serious disruptions to the city. Almost overnight many government contracts, including those for Aircraft Engines, were cancelled. The immediate effect was massive layoffs of the thousands employed in the many factories in Paterson and surrounding towns.

Beginning in late 1945 and continuing through 1946 thousands of service veterans were returning to the city and suburbs. They all needed housing and jobs, both of which were in very short supply. The city did respond with several crash programs to build veterans housing to ease that crisis. The job availability was a much more challenging problem that took several years to resolve.

Abbott Brothers

514 Totowa Ave Mill 1940 to 1960

Mc Bride Ave Mill 1921 to 1940

Abbott Bros. was the business that my grandfather George J Abbott and his brother Francis W Abbott (aka 'Uncle Frank") started in 1906. The Brothers were both emigres from England that came to the United States in the latter half of the nineteenth century. They initially worked for one of the many Ribbon Mills that operated in Paterson at the time before establishing their own business.

The Abbott Brothers had an interesting history. The two brothers married two sisters. After they married almost simultaneously, they purchased a two-family house at 488 Union Ave. They each had a floor to start and raise their families.

My Grandfather, George Abbott and his wife Martha Lister had three sons who grew up there. Uncle Frank (Francis W Abbott) and his wife Ida had two daughters that grew up here as well.

The brothers enjoyed early and sustained success. Despite their success, they lived quite frugally. For example, they shared one telephone for both families that was on a table in the commonly shared front hall. They did this for fifty plus years! In addition, they also shared a car that was only ever driven by my dad. The first car, a Hupmoble was purchased around 1912 and was only used in the spring, summer, and fall. In the winter the car was put up on blocks in the garage they owned on Kearny Street.

My Dad, Stuart Abbott became a partner in the Mill in the early thirties. Uncle Franks son-in-law Joseph H Buckley also became a partner around the same time.It is interesting to note that this small narrow fabric weaving mill sustained four families in a comfortable middle class existence for forty plus years.

In the good years the mill operated both a day and a night shift. With over forty employees there was never a successful union election in the mill.

This is a testament to the reasonable and fair treatment of the employees that I and my siblings are understandably proud of. We all learned valuable lessons from our dad that served us well in our own ventures later in life.

My three brothers and I all worked in the mill after school and on Saturday mornings. Our early jobs usually involved filling the Fire Pails mounted on numerous columns, making reels for the finished ribbon, and burning the trash on Saturday mornings in the "Incinerator".

This was a real exaggeration as it was nothing more than a few sections of cyclone fencing cobbled together to contain the fire. It was really a very basic contraption and today I laugh whenever I hear the word "incinerator".

As we got older the kids would graduate to more skilled jobs such as Skein Winding that prepared the Ribbon for dyeing, Quill winding and "Blocking" which was winding the dyed ribbon on to one-hundred-yard reels.

Saturday mornings were a wonderful time working in the Mill. We got to spend real quality time with my dad. The best part was when work ended at noon, and we would go to Taylors Meat Pies on Union Ave near Kearny Street and get a dozen Meat Pies for Saturday lunch. I have had the pleasure of enjoying a lot of good meals in my life, but none were better than Taylors Meat ("Mutton") pies for Saturday lunch.

Taylor's Meat ("Mutton") Pies

Chichi's Luncheonette, August, 1969

Taylors Storenext to Chichi's on Union Avenue

Hillcrest & The Totowa Section

I grew up in the Hillcrest section of Paterson. In the forties and fifties when Hillcrest consisted of well-maintained homes inhabited by all white residents. They were primarily of European decent and either second, or third generation Americans. With two large Roman Catholic parishes available within walking distance the church's influence was quite dominant. One of my neighbors, Dot Hanstein, became a nun during this time and one of my close pals growing up, Joey Hertel, became a Franciscan Priest after going to St Bonaventure's Elementary, High School and University. My Aunts, Uncles, and cousins in addition to my immediate family were the token Protestants on Emerson Avenue.

While growing up my mother in particular constantly reminded us that we lived in "Hillcrest" and we were very privileged to live in one of Paterson's best neighborhoods that was clearly one of the richest and definitely one of the safest places to grow up.

My family had five children and most of our neighbors had two or three kids. Many of our neighbors worked in public service.

There were three policemen, a fire chief, and a mailman living in one block of Emerson Avenue between Totowa and Union Avenues. Crime was nonexistent.

The other neighbor Dads were a combination of skilled tradesmen, professionals such as teachers, Doctors, and middle managers along with several small business owners.

With only occasional exceptions for limited part time work, most of the mothers were the classic stay at home moms. There were no "latch key" kids, no day care issues, no pre-school and certainly no "pre-K".

Society sure has evolved from this bucolic existence, but probably not for the better.

We did not know it at the time but life on Emerson Avenue during these years was the quintessential American Dream. The Saturday Evening Post could have done covers based on our life here.

During the Holiday Season of 1953/1954 Hillcrest had a tragedy intrude on this bucolic period. The Ench family lived in a large restored historic home on the corner of Totowa and

Arlington Avenue. Every Christmas Emma Ench would create a large holiday display in the ground floor basement of her home. The display was titled, "The Land of Let's Believe". The figures in each of the fairy tale scenes were miniature porcelain dolls imported from Germany. They were all dressed in costumes hand made by Emma Ench.

After New Years and just before the display was disassembled, she would traditionally host a party for the younger children of the neighborhood. During the party the children were roasting marshmallows in the large open fireplace. While one of the children was waving a flaming marshmallow, the live, now very dry, decorations caught fire. The entire room was quickly engulfed in flames. The children were all immediately evacuated to the first-floor kitchen and exited the home safely. MsEnch was injured and was found barely alive on the stairway. Unfortunately, she passed away the following day. The girl in the picture is my cousin Leslie Mills (Saglibene). My brother George Abbott and another cousin Bob Skelton were also at this party. While tragic, that day's event could easily have been a much larger disaster. Everyone involved that day got a very early life lesson in the fragility of life.

About 1953 at Emma Ench's Christmas displays at 95 Totowa Ave.

Cousin Leslie Mills (Saglibene) and my brother

George Abbott with Ms. Ench

STOP PAYING RENT!
Visit This Ideal Home

1939

NEW HOMES
HILLCREST AREA

ELBERON AVE
NEAR
TOTOWA AVE
PATERSON

10% DOWN   **$34.20 Monthly**   10% DOWN
Total Carrying Charges

Air-Conditioned
Domestic Science Kitchen

All Improvements
In and Paid For

RIVERVIEW HOMES, INC.
ELBERON AND EMERSON AVES.
Between Totowa and Union Aves., Paterson
OPEN DAILY   LAMBERT 3-8581

Advertisement for the Development where I lived.

NICK & CHARLIE'S RESTAURANT
THE RED BAR
LUNCHEONS - DINNERS
CHOICE WINES - LIQUORS - BEERS

FAMILY
DINNERS
PIZZA
SIZZLING
STEAKS

AIR - CONDITIONED

Catering For Weddings - Banquets
Office Parties - Private Dinning Room
Open Every Day - Sundays
Dial **279 - 0287**
365 Totowa Ave. Paterson, N.J.
(Cer. of Wayne Ave.)

A Long Time Favorite Bar & Restaurant in The Totowa Section

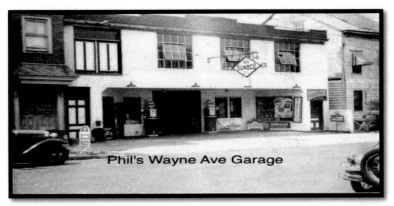

Phil's Wayne Ave Garage

My "Go to" place for Gas and Car Repairs in the 50's (Because the purchases went on dad's account)

The Beautiful Hillcrest Home of Dr Archie Ged on Union and

Emerson Avenue

Hinchcliffe Stadium – The Old & The New

After the Great Falls Hincliffe Stadium is probably one of Paterson's most distinguishing landmarks. It was built in the middle of the great depression in 1932 with assistance from the WPA. The "Works Progress Administration" was a depression era organization that provided jobs for the massive number of unemployed residents.

The original capacity was 10,000 seats. In its new, 2023 rehabilitated configuration the capacity is 7,500 seats.

Baseball:

The stadium is one of the last remaining Negro League stadiums in the United States. It is the first one designated as a National Historic Landmark Honoring Baseball and the only venue within the boundary of a National Park. Over 20 Hall of Fame players graced Hinchcliffe's hallowed grounds with many having played in the Negro Leagues.

Hinchcliffe's horseshoe style configuration is similar to the Polo Grounds, the longtime home of baseball's New York Giants and the NFL's football Giants. After opening to great fanfare in 1932 the sports promotors of the day quickly noticed that when visiting African American ball clubs played at Hinchcliffe, the attendance would increase.

Over time the stadium would serve as the home park for the New York Black Yankees, New York Cubans an occasional the Newark Eagles.

It is interesting to note that the tradition of "New York" named teams playing their games in New Jersey stadiums is not new in the current era but goes back to 1932.

In 1942, Larry Doby, a new graduate of Paterson's Eastside High School was offered a tryout with the Newark Eagles at the stadium. Doby made the ball club; a day would change his life forever. On July 5, 1947, Doby made his Major League Baseball debut with the Cleveland Indians as he first African American player in the American League, a short 11 weeks after Jackie Robinson had integrated the National League.

The stadium was designated a National Historic Landmark in March 2013and became a Paterson Historic Landmark in May 2013. In December of 2014 Congress passed a resolution to include the stadium in the Great Falls National Landmark District.

After an extensive restoration in 2023 Hinchcliffe is again hosting Paterson High School sports and is the home of the New Jersey Jackals of the Frontier League minor league baseball team. The reconstruction also added a 315-space parking garage, a fast-food court, an interpretive center, and a Senior Citizen Housing complex.

In the course of its long history Hincliffe has hosted many professional and amateur event categories including:

- Baseball
- Football
- Boxing
- Midget and Stock Car Racing
- Motorcycle Racing
- Jack Kochman's "Hell Drivers"

The year 1933 would mark the Black Yankees' first visit to Paterson. They took on The Gavin Pros, a white professional team playing the games at Hinchcliffe Stadium.

The Gavins were not the only team to call Hinchcliffe home. A team called the Paterson City Club also played at Hinchcliffe against high profile ball clubs such as the Pittsburgh Pirates, The Baltimore Black Sox, Chief Bender's House of David, and the Oklahoma Indians who were led by football hall of famer Jim Thorpe.

Over time the Paterson City Club folded, leaving only the Gavins to play at Hinchcliffe. The local promoters noticed that attendance would increase when the local professionals would play against black teams. Subsequently they invited the New York

Black Yankees to play their home games in the 1933 National Colored Championship series versus the Pittsburg Crawfords at Hinchcliffe. They played a five-game series over a 15-day span between Paterson and Pittsburgh.

The Black Yankees provided many memorable moments at Hinchcliffe including:

- The Black Yankees started their 1934 season at the stadium with an eight-game winning streak that was halted by none other than Hall of Famer Josh Gibson.
- In a game against the Nashville Elite Giants 200 orphans were in attendance to see the Black Yankees play at Hinchcliffe.
- Ten days after winning the 1934 World Series, the Brooklyn Farm Team with Hall of Famer Dizzy Dean and his brother Daffy played against the Black Yankees.

Larry Doby

Active Player
1947 - 1959

From
Paterson, NJ

OUTFIELD   CLEVELAND INDIANS®

No history of Hincliffe Stadium and Paterson Sports would be complete without recognizing Larry Doby and his amazing accomplishments. Born Lawrence Eugene Doby in Camden, South Carolina, he moved to Paterson at the age of 14 and graduated from Eastside High School. Doby's athletic prowess earned him Varsity Letters in four sports: basketball, football, track and of course, baseball.

Soon after graduating from Eastside in 1942, Doby was offered a tryout with the Newark Eagles. At the suggestion of a Negro League umpire, Eagles owner Abe Manley agreed to give Doby a try outright after the Eagles were in town to play the New York Black Yankees at Hinchcliffe.

In typical Doby fashion, he excelled at the try outIn his home ballpark and played the rest of the summer with the Newark Eagles. Years later at his Hall of Fame induction in 1998, Doby cited that tryout with the Eagles as his most memorable moment at Hinchcliffe Stadium.

His time in Newark was cut short as he served in the Navy from 1943 until being honorably discharged in January of 1946.

While he was serving in Ulithi in the western Pacific Doby heard over Armed Forces Radio about the Brooklyn Dodgers signing Jackie Robinson. He and Robinson would eventually integrate into major league baseball in 1947.

On July 4, 1947,Larry Doby played his final game in an Eagles uniform. Between games of a double header Doby was informed that the Cleveland Indians purchased his contract. After the news leaked to the press Doby joined the club while they were on a road trip to Chicago. When Doby arrived there, he was not allowed to stay at the team's hotel.

After a long train trip Doby made his Major League debut on July 5, 1947, thus becoming the first African American in the American League. In his first game he was asked to pinch hit and struck out.

This was not surprising since he had just taken a long train ride, playing a game the previous day, and being given the cold shoulder after being diverted to Chicago.

After changing positions from the infield to the outfield and an offseason of intense development Doby left Spring Training in 1948 as the starting right fielder for the ball club. By mid-June he had moved to center field, a position he would hold for most of his career.

Dobie hit .301 in his first full season in the majors which culminated with the Indians winning the 1948 World Series. After hitting a crucial home run in game four of the series starting pitcher Steve Gromek was photographed with Doby in a full-on embrace. This was probably the first of many sports pictures showing a black player and a white player hugging each other.

Larry Doby receiving a Key to The City from Mayor Michael U DeVita

Football

While Baseball marked the time at Hincliffe, the stadium was really built for football. In 1930 the famed Thanksgiving Day clash between archrivals Central and Eastside High Schools was played on a parcel of available land near the Great Falls. That football field was graded on the exact location where Hinchcliffe Stadium stands today.

Temporary seating was erected on that cold yet auspicious Thanksgiving in 1930. The stadium would become a reality and open its doors to the public on July 8, 1932.

Almost as soon as the local athletes dug their cleats into the new stadium turf in 1932, Hinchcliffe was declared the home stadium to no less than three professional football teams: The Silk City Bears, The Paterson Giants, and the Paterson Nighthawks. Hinchcliffe would soon become the home of the well-known Paterson Panthers in 1934. They played at Hinchcliffe continuously through 1950, except for a break during WWII.

In 1936 the Panthers joined the newly formed American Professional Football Association (APFA). On September 24, 1939, The panthers faced the Brooklyn Eagles team that included a player by the name of Vince Lombardi who later became the famed coach of the Green Bay Packers and the Washington Redskins.

After fours of downtime during World War II, the Panthers returned to Hinchcliffe from 1946 to 1950.

In 1947 the Panthers had a successful season and hosted the American Professional Football League championship game at Hinchcliffe Stadium. The Bethlehem Bulldogs were crowned champions in a 23–7 rout of Paterson in front of a crowd of 10,587.

In 1948 the Paterson Panthers redeemed themselves and were crowned American Football League Champions after defeating the Wilmington Clippers by a score of 24-14 in front of a crowd of over 10,000 fans.

At the time Paterson's coach was Allie Sherman. The 1948 season was Shermans first year as the coach after a five-year career as a professional player. His time in Paterson was short-lived as he was offered a position with the New York Football Giants as their Running Backs Coach. He would later become the head coach of the Giants from 1961 to 1968.

Thanksgiving Traditions: Thanksgiving was virtually Hinchcliffe's reason for being, for the locals it has remained a large part of its reason for being remembered. The first ever Thanksgiving Day Classic in the new stadium resulted in Central High School defeating Eastside 24-0.

The annual game between Eastside and Central (Kennedy HS beginning in 1964) is one of the oldest rivalry games in the state of New Jersey that continues today.

On Thanksgiving Day 1941, Eastside player, Larry Doby, gave his Central High School counterparts severe indigestion with 45-6 drubbing in front of 12,500 spectators.

On that day, Doby participated in every way imaginable. Not only did he score two touchdowns, but he also had a snap at quarterback and threw a pass to set up a touchdown on the ensuing play, returning a kickoff for 32 yards and then kicking the extra point.

Boxing

Boxing came to Hinchcliffe in the late 1930's, another opportunity for tough, poor kids to show their stuff that quickly evolved into a family spectator sport. By the late 1930's the stadium was already hosting Diamond Gloves Championship bouts, predecessor to the Golden Gloves. Paterson's own Lou Duva won a championship here in 1940 in the bantam weight Division. Later, as a world class trainer and promoter, Duva built a career that produced other champions.

Paterson native Lou Costello, the legendary Hollywood comic, was also a serious boxing enthusiast. Well into the 1940's Costello could be found at Diamond Glove bouts with his pal Duva and their mutual friend Gaetano Federici, whose sculptures of Costello, Ingrid Bergman, and "Jack Dempsey's Arms" had made him the de facts culptor of the stars.

The bouts were guest refereed by boxing champions Jack Dempsey in '43 and Joe Louis in '49. They then socialized in the stadium with sports celebrities like Babe Ruth, Pee Wee Reese, Herman Franks, Max Baer, Sugar Ray Robinson, Joe Louis, Rocky Graziano, Rocky Marciano, Jake LaMotta, and Dixie

Walker. Larry Doby and other Paterson stars would often come back to Hinchcliffe to see and be seen at major boxing events. They would find themselves sharing the limelight with superstars of screen and radio.

It should be noted that in 1946it was the semifinals of the Diamond Gloves Championships at Hinchcliffe that made sports history as the first telecast of an athletic event on July 31,1946.

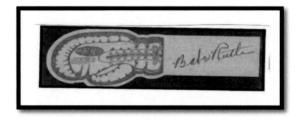

Racing

A year and a half after Hinchcliffe Stadium opened, a new sport was introduced to Patersonians. A man by the name of Ed Otto, appeared before the Stadium Commissioners to propose and idea. He wanted to stage motorcycle meets and midget car races. He offered $150 a night for the guaranteed rental. (Approximately $2,910 in today's dollars. Years later Ed Otto became one of the founders of NASCAR.

On June 5, 1934, motorsports made its debut on Hinchcliffe Stadium's cinder track. The first motorsport event was a motorcycle race featuring a 17-event program that crowned Canadian Champion Crocky Rawding as the new US Champion. Goldie Restall, the 1932 Motorcycle Speed Racing Champion of the Eastern United States, also appeared in the first race and did four laps in one minute and 18 seconds!

A mere two months later, Otto and his partner John "Jack" Kotchman, introduced midget car racing to Hinchcliffe's roster of events. While the motorcycle races were immediately successful drawing crowds of over 11,000 patrons, the infancy of midget car racing had several false starts. The early days of midget car racing were a bit disorganized at Hinchcliffe as the sport was new to east coast drivers.

Paterson's Gasoline Alley came to the rescue of midget car racing at the stadium, Located on East 29th Street Gasoline Alley began as a series of auto repair shops in the 1920's. With the advent of racing at Hinchcliffe, it became a mecca for professional drivers to refine their race cars. Several legendary racers such as Roscoe" Pappy" Hough and Ted Horn were regulars at Gasoline Alley. Hough built his famed "five little pigs" team of cars at Gasoline Alley and Horn was a three-time AAA National Championship winner in 1946-48.

The stadium and Gasoline Alley put Paterson on the midget car racing Map. Other motor sports would find a home at Hinchcliffe Stadium as well. Ed Otto would continue to work his magic and was an integral part in establishing stock car racing at Hinchcliffe.

After that John "Jack" Kotchman brought his own brand of automotive entertainment under the name "Jack Kotchman's Hell Drivers". Kotchman's exhibitions drew very well at Hinchcliffe with thrilling stunts and death-defying acts were the norm in his presentations.

From motorcycle racing to Hell Drivers, Hinchcliffe had a full share of motorsports thrills. The stadium's racing history also had national implications as many events featured East Coast vs West Coast competitions. "Bronco" Bill Schindler and Art Cross had the most victories in Hinchcliffe history, Schindler with 52 wins and Cross with 47. Both are members of the National Midget Racing Hall of Fame.

Midget Car Racers at Hinchcliffe Stadium

Pappy Hough's "5 Little Pigs" traveling racing community in 1947. Left to right, Dee Toran, Jeep Colkitt, Red Raymond, Roscoe "Pappy" Hough, and Walt Walasek.

Rosco 'Pappy' Hough

Gasoline Alley 1938

Miget Car Racing at Hinchcliffe Stadium

Stock Car Racing at Hinchcliffe Stadium

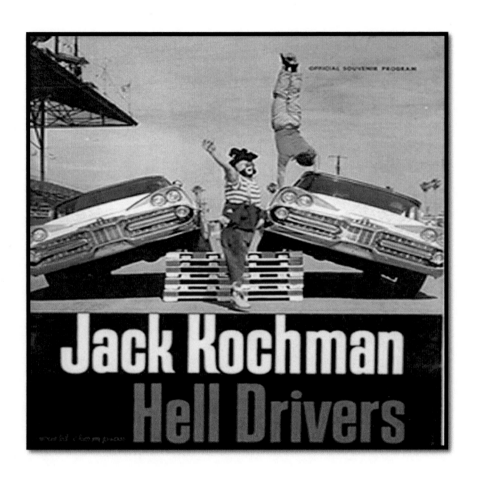

The One & Only Kack Kochman's Hell Drivers

Stock Car Auto Races

OFFICIAL PROGRAM

HINCHLIFFE STADIUM
PATERSON, N. J.

Hot Texas Wieners

An Absolute Classic: In the "One All The Way" variation

The precise details are lost in time, but the father of the original "Hot Texas Wiener" was John Petrellis, a Greek immigrant who settled in Paterson in the early 1900's.

Petrellis worked for his uncle, who had lived for a short time in Texas before moving to Paterson. He then opened a hot dog stand in the now-defunct Manhattan Hotel on Paterson Street. (Now Memorial Drive) At the other end of the block a joint called Tarapada's boasted the hottest chili in town. Rounding out the Paterson Street businesses were nine all-night bars.

Between those salt hot dogs and that blazing chili, it must have taken the combined pouring power of all nine bars to keep the "flames" under control.

At his Paterson Street hot dog stand Petrellis had a customer who would regularly bring his chili to the stand to put on his hot dogs. Shortly after Petrellis began serving his hot dogs topped with this chili.

Now all the necessary ingredients were in place for the Hot Texas Wiener to come into existence: Tarapada's spicy chili, Petrellis's uncle's Texas influence and of course the deep-fried wieners. A true gastronomic classic was born.

Throughout the balance of the twentieth century and now into the twenty first a large number of "Hot Texas Wiener" joints were established in Paterson and the surrounding towns of Clifton, Totowa Boro, Fairlawn and Hawthorne. The vast majority were started and operated by either Greek immigrants, or their next generation offspring.

In 1940 John Petrellis opened the Olympic Grill on Mc Bride Avenue directly across the famous Libby's Lunch operated by William Pappas. The Bettses family leased the Olympic Grill from John Petrellis and gained the necessary experience that would later evolve into the hugely successful Falls View Grill.

In subsequent years many copycat operations began operations that had their own share of success and expanded the market for the signature "Hot Texas Wiener".

In the mid-forties my dad's mill was then located on Mc Bride Avenue almost directly across the street from Libby's. I was probably about seven years old when on a Saturday morning visit to the mill my dad took me across the street to Libby's for lunch. That day started a lifelong love affair with the "Hot Texas Wiener" in the "All the Way" configuration. That means the deep-fried wiener is topped with yellow mustard, chopped onions and a generous amount of highly proprietary chili sauce.

In my 42-year business career I have spent over twenty years living far from New Jersey, primarily in Southern California and the Chicago Illinois area. Believe me the Chicago Hot Dog is a decent version of a deep-fried hot dog, but neither it, nor the "Chili Dogs" of Detroit and Cincinnati are a match for Paterson's classic Hot Texas Wiener.

During my away years in California and Illinois I would regularly manage to use business trips to buy containers of the highly proprietary chili sauce, usually from the Hot Grill, and bring them home. They were then carefully rationed out to get the maximum number of Hot Texas Wieners.

By my unscientific count there were 12 businesses making the signature Hot Texas Wieners in Paterson during the fifties when my consumption was at its peak. The following pictures will hopefully trigger a memory, or two for those who were fortunate enough to have the experience of "Two all the way, Frenchy well done, sometimes with gravy."

Unique Foods of Paterson

P aterson has been a true "melting pot" of nationalities and cultures for many years. One of the most wonderful benefits of growing up in this environment was the variety and quantity of ethnic foods that were readily available throughout the city.

In my personal experience Italian food was probably the most dominant. However, I was also exposed to Greek, Syrian, German, Scotch and Jewish cuisine. My waistline is living proof of just how much I enjoyed this food bonanza in my hometown.

The Greek influence was and is pervasive throughout the city as evidenced by the number of Hot Texas Wiener Shops. The Italian food availability is city wide and not neighborhood specific. Syrian food and baked goods were heavily concentrated in the South Paterson area. Neither the Scotch, nor the German food was confined to a specific neighborhood. Jewish food was definitely a big part of the Eastside neighborhoods.

The latter category has a special meaning for me. My mother-in-law and I both worked part time at Kanter's Deli and liquor store. I loved my Saturday mornings with Al Morris and

MaxNisenholtz, the de facto Mayor of the Eastside, who always had the latest news, gossip, and stories to share. My love of Bagels, Bialy's, Cream Cheese & Lox, Corned Beef and Pastrami really started right here on Broadway on Paterson's Eastside.

Max Nisenholtz and The Kanter's Crew

In the late 40's and early 50's there was a caterer in Paterson by the name of Hap Nightingale. Hap had a very large niche business with churches, veteran's organizations, volunteer fire companies and other organizations that hire him to cater his legendary Beefsteak Dinners. His formula was elegantly simple. He would roast large cuts of serious prime beef and while it was still rare to medium rare, slice it quite thin, dip it in melted garlic butter and then layer it on plain untoasted white bread. No frills, just one or two side dishes and loads of sliced beef drenched in butter on White bread. They were served buffet style and were always "all you can eat" affairs.

Hap's success spawned numerous copycats, including Dr Phil Provisiero of the Paterson Exchange Club who did numerous that I sometimes had the privilege of attending with my parents and siblings.

The quintessential "Beefsteak Dinner - Hap style"

Pizza

In the late 40's this pure English heritage kid was introduced to the joy of a Paterson Pizza. That early experience quickly bloomed into what has been a lifelong love affair with what many originally called "Tomatoe Pie".

I have eaten pizza In more than ten US States, Naples, Italy and Palermo, Sicily. None of them can compare to those served up by my 40's and 50's Paterson Favorites: Casa Rosa, Shepi's, Patsy's Tavern, and my Hillcrest favorite, Joe's Pizzeria on Union, and Berkshire Avenues.

A Classic Plain Pizza from Patsy's Tavern

Casa Rosa Home of Awesome Pizza & Mussels

Bakeries

For a city of its size Paterson in the 40's and 50's had more bakeries and a greater variety of bakery specialties than any other New Jersey city. There were numerous shops making only Italian Bread and Rolls. Ther well-known names of the day were Lazzara's and Giannelli's. Other Italian bakers offered awesome cakes and pastries. The Paterson Pastry Shop and Totowa Pastry were two I have patronized for their awesome offerings. There were several German Heritage bakeries scattered throughout the city. South Paterson had a significant Syrian bakery presence.

A few of the Italian Bread and Roll Bakers offered full line delicatessens to complement their baked goods.

Stores like Giannella's, and Minardi's were the go-to places for not only bread and rolls, but the best imported cold cuts, salads, and Italian Specialty foods. Today the supermarket deli departments now dominate this market but cannot compare to those old-line family run shops.

The Swiss Bakery on Ellison St.

GRAND REOPENING
TOMORROW
PETER TOMASI & SONS
PROSPECT BAKERY

Alterations-Remodeling Having Just Been Completed
Tasty Old-Fashioned Hearth Oven Baked
ITALIAN-FRENCH BREAD & ROLLS
INTRODUCING
NEW LINE FANCY CAKES & COOKIES

59 PROSPECT ST.   PATERSON
PHONE SHER. 2-1904
—ESTABLISHED 40 YEARS—

Ice Cream

Paterson unique foods is not complete without some discussion of two of my all-time favorites, Country Club Ice Cream and Boonstra's Dairy.

Country Club was manufactured at their plant in the Hillcrest section was in my experience the absolute best ice cream ever produced. It preceded Ben & Jerry's, Haagen Dazs, and other premium brands. They competed with Breyers, Borden's, and Hershey's, but it was no contest. Paterson's Guernsey Crest was another premium brand made in the city that in personal judgment was a close second to Country Club. Unfortunately, the Country Club business was sold to Hood Dairies of Boston who moved production out of the city and into a rapid slide to mediocrity.

Fortunately, Guernsey Crest has weathered several storms and continues to operate.

Boonstra's Dairy was just three short blocks from where I grew up on Emerson Avenue. Their home-made ice cream was also a premier quality product on a par with Country Club. During my late wife's pregnancy, she probably consumed over 40 hand packed half pints of Boonstra's Chocolate Ice Cream. Fortunately, they were very close to our home at the time.

The Boonstra's made another product that brought a steady stream of customers to their Union Avenue store. Their home-made Buttermilk was like nothing else available and would have been a real no-no in today's Cholesterol conscious world. FYI: Boonstra's was on the border of Paterson and Totowa Boro, but they were in Paterson, not Totowa.

Meat Pies AKA: "Mutton Pies":

No food of Paterson is more unique than the Meat Pie better known as the "Mutton Pie". They were very popular with immigrant textile workers from England and Scotland in the early 1900's

In the early days they really did use Mutton, or Lamb as the main component in the filling mixture. Since the beginning of WWII, the filling has used a ground beef-based filling. The unique hand shaped crust is also beef flavored.

The Taylor family made their version of the Scotch pie for over 65 years. Today there is no Taylor Meat Pies available as the last members of the family have retired. However, comparable meat pies are still available from Scotch shops in Kearney and Brick, New Jersey.

This delectable treat was a staple on my family's table every Saturday as I was growing up in the 40's & 50's. I sure do miss them.

Staff photo by Ed Hill

Al Taylor: "We've used the same ingredients ... [for] as long as I can remember."

Meat pies to drive for

Swimming Spots

In the largely un-air-conditioned world of North Jersey in the 40's and 50's kids were preoccupied with going to a place where they could swim and stay wet in the steamy weather.

Fortunately for young Paterson boys there was a readily accessible swimming spot available at the Paterson YMCA. The "Y" had a very large pool that was open year-round and provided swimming lessons, as well as the opportunity to swim competitively. My brother Don and I along with our neighbors, the Hertel's all learned to swim well during many Saturdays at the "Y".I had the privilege of being on the "Y" Swimming Team that won the YMCA Central Atlantic Area Championship in 1951 at the Princeton University Pool.

The Paterson YMCA – An awesome facility with a top notchgym and a state of the art pool. Paterson's kids are truly blessed to have this facility available.

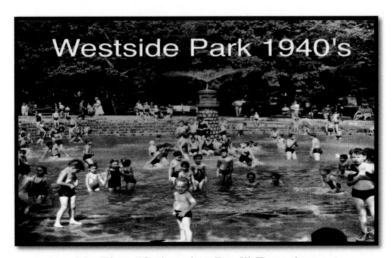

My First "Swimming Pool" Experience

My Swimming Spots in & around Paterson in the 40's & 50's:

- Circle Pool in Paterson
- Preakness Pool in Totowa Boro
- Hinchman's in Wayne
- Lakeside Pool in Haledon
- Suntan Lake in Riverdale
- Terrace Lake in Butler
- Mc Donalds Beach I n Pequannock
- Forest Hill Park in West Milford
- Mullers Piond in Oakland
- Ernie Nees' Valley Springs Lake in Riverdale
- Palisades Park in Palisades Park

VERFS PRESENTS SUGARCANE FRI SAT

SUN TAN LAKE

CATERING   MINIATURE GOLF   COCKTAIL LOUNGE

SWIMMING   BOATING   PICNIC AREAS

S' VALLEY SPRING LAKE, a unique spring-fed l
r always going over the dam. Shady picnic gr
ern refreshment stand. West of Riverdale circl
te 23. E. Nees, Jr. Phone Butler 9-0836.

Three Great Swimming Spots: Palisades Park, Ernie Nees'
Valley Spring Lake in Riverdale& Suntan Lake in Butler

Paterson Movie Theaters

D uring the period we are reviewing Paterson had an inordinate number of Movie Houses when the city's Population was approximately 140,000. Since television sets did not become a common household appliance until the fifties it is easy to understand why ten theaters could survive and prosper, particularly since their admission price was one of the best entertainment values available.

OLD PATERSON THEATERS OF THE 50S

Capitol Theater - 368 21st Ave.
Fabian Theatre - 45 Church St.
Garden Theatre - 204 Market St.
Majestic Theater - 293 Main St.
Plaza Theater - 435 Union Ave.
Rivoli Theatre - 130 Main St.
Rialto Theater - 999 Main St.
State Theatre - 61 Van Houten St.
U.S. Theatre - 284 Main St.
Regent Theatre - 12 Union St. (Now Veterans Pl.)

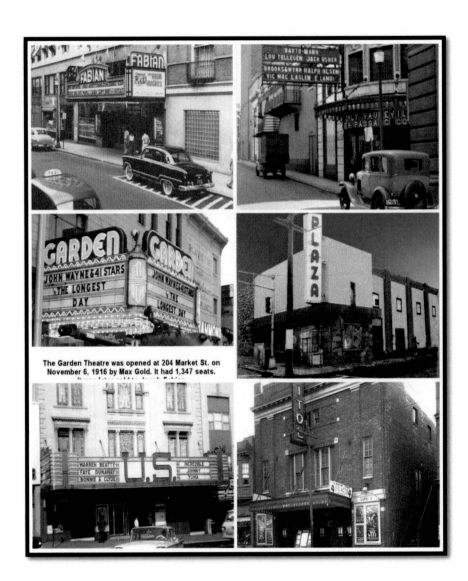

The Garden Theatre was opened at 204 Market St. on
November 6, 1916 by Max Gold. It had 1,347 seats.

The "Clan" and Cliff's Store

The "Clan" was the chosen nickname for a group of eleven teenagers who would get together almost daily at Cliff's Variety Store and Soda Fountain on Union Ave between Edmund and Preakness Avenues. The choice of the word "clan" as our group nickname was probably influenced by the Scotch, Irish and English heritage of many in the group.

The "Clan" Members included: Don Abbott, Stu McKinley, Billy McKinley, Al Titus, Art Messenger, Gus Peters, CraigBradley, Ronnie Baker, Bob Campbell, Al Capter and of course, Doug Abbott.

Our group and meeting location was very similar to two other similar spots on Union Ave: Netzers and the Totowa Spa.

Netzers was frequented primarily by students at St. Mary's High School and the Totowa Spa had several groups who met up there regularly.

Cliffs had several features that made it attractive to our group. First, Cliff the owner was very often an absentee manager, leaving the store in the hands of Gus Peters, one of the "Clan" Members.

Equally important in the pre cell phone era the store had a classic New Jersey Bell Telephone Company phone booth that did not have a lot of users. The guys in the "Clan" treated it as their private phone line. During the five plus years that I was part of the "Clan" I probably dropped over a hundred dollars in quarters into this pay phone.

Another great feature of Cliff's was the large, vintage Soda Fountain stocked with many flavors of Breyer's Ice Cream. With Gus Peters behind the counter our Shakes, Malteds, Ice Cream Soda's and Sundaes were always "super-sized". Fortunately, personal weight was not an issue for any of us in those days. That curse would come later in life.

The many hours spent with the guys at Cliff's were another large and important part of the wonderful life that we all experienced in the fifties. It was the absolute local personification of the "Happy Days experience" and we lived it to the fullest.

Top 1957 Hits

1. All Shook Up - Elvis Presley
2. Love Letters In Sand - Pat Boone
3. Little Darlin' - The Diamonds
4. Young Love - Tab Hunter
5. So Rare - Jimmy Dorsey
6. Don't Forbid Me - Pat Boone
7. Singing the Blues - Guy Mitchell
8. Young Love - Sonny James
9. Too Much - Elvis Presley
10. Round And Round - Perry Como
11. Bye Bye Love - The Everly Brothers
12. Tammy - Debbie Reynolds
13. Party Doll - Buddy Knox
14. (Let Me Be Your) Teddy Bear - Elvis Presley
15. Banana Boat Song (Day-O) - Harry Belafonte
16. Jailhouse Rock - Elvis Presley
17. A White Sport Coat (And a Pink Carnation) - Marty Robbins
18. Come Go With Me - The Del Vikings
20. You Send Me - Sam Cooke

Good Ol' Days

Netzers

Totowa Spa, Union & Wayne Ave.-1938

An Exact Copy of the Phone Booth in Cliff's Store

Linwal's & The Haledon Diner

I n addition to providing good food the many diners of North Jersey were natural gathering places for families, friends, and many groups of teenagers. The Haledon Diner on Belmont Avenue in Haledon was right on the Paterson border and very conveniently accessible for not only residents of the city, but also the surrounding suburbs. Most importantly it was open on a 24/7 schedule.

For an eight-year period from 1951 to 1959 it was my go-to place when I was looking for my friends and potential dates. It was also the place to go after a night out on some social activity and dates. Fortunately, our dates did not know that the gang at the diner would regularly engage in after date critiques. These discussions could be very humorous, shocking and at times cruel. They were never repeated to anyone who was not part of the group chat.

All the diners of this era had a jukebox. One of our favorite activities was to find a song that would either annoy, or embarrass a friend, and we would then play that song repeatedly and of course get a lot of laughs in the process.

At one of the late nights get togethers my younger brother Don came into the diner with a new date. After we were introduced, I couldn't help but admire him for his good taste. Their relationship fortunately for me did not last, but about two years later I married that girl and stayed married to her for fifty-seven years.

The diner had another feature beyond its food that appealed to those guys that were inclined to gamble. There were two state of the art pin ball machines in an alcove near the restrooms. There was a "secret" schedule of scores that would pay off a cash prize of $5.00 to $25.00.

It would be an understatement to say that these prizes were not easy to win. One of my best friends in DeMolay was really addicted to these machines. He would spend hours pouring nickels by the roll into these machines. Fortunately, he got over the gambling thing and would go on to become the President of a large Printing Ink company.

Linwal's was a small restaurant on Rt 46 at the Rt 46 & Rt 23 Circle in Wayne prior to Rt 80 being built. They had awesome Open Grilled Hamburgers, Cheeseburgers as well as homemade donuts. Me and my friends from the Cliff's Union Avenue store "Clan" have literally eaten at Linwal's hundreds of times between 1952 and 1959.

To be honest it was not just the food at Linwal's that was the primary attraction. There were usually two, or three waitresses on a shift. Jack and Bill the owners of Linwal's lived in Packanack Lake. There had to be an incredible number of great looking girls living there because there was never hired any waitress who was not a nine, or a ten on a scale of one to ten. The competition for dates with these girls was fierce. I'm not sure what my "batting average" was, but I was not anywhere near a .300 hitter.

However, there is a beautiful end to the Linwal's saga. I dated a Linwal's waitress by the name of Kathi Marshall in 1958 and 1959 while I was in the Navy and after I was discharged. For several reasons our relationship did not last long term. However, some 62 years later I got a text message from Kathi Marshal Kazanjian who was now a widow living in Foley, Alabama.

She came across my contact information in my Facebook Profile. I was also a widower for about a year at the time. After a lot of telephone calls, we began to fill in the gaps of our lives for the those 62 missing years. After a visit to Foley and a return visit to my New Jersey home the decision was made in the fall of 2021 for me to relocate to Foley, Alabama. Now, almost two years later we have a wonderful relationship and are living the good life on Lower Alabama's Gulf Coast. A sincere thank you to Facebook and social media for making it all possible.

DeMolay

The order of DeMolay had a profound impact on my teenage years and subsequent years. Two of my brothers were members as were most of my closest friends. All of us were heavily influenced by our fathers who were active members of various local Masonic lodges that sponsored the Paterson DeMolay Chapter.

The order of DeMolay teaches seven core values including: Filial Love, Reverence, Courtesy, Comradeship, Fidelity, Cleanness, and Patriotism.

In the 40's and 50's the Paterson Chapter of DeMolay was a very vibrant and active organization with a largetypical membership roster of over fifty teenaged boys between the ages of twelve and twenty-one.

There were also several adult men who mentored and guided the chapter rituals and social activities.

In an average year the National organization of Demolay awards $160,000 in scholarships, donates $72,000 to charity and contributes 6,200+ hours of Community Service.

An annual Paterson DeMolay Installation in The Mid Fifties

The Paterson Masonic Temple on Broadway

The Paterson Masonic Club & DeMolay Club Rooms

The Masonic Club is the social activity center for the various Lodges that meet in Paterson Temple. In the early fifties our DeMolay Chapter was offered the use of the vacant third floor of the Club for recreational purposes. The hitch was that the rooms were in a state of disrepair and would need a lot of work to make them functional. With a lot of donations of time, labor, paint, furniture and carpeting we were able to make the rooms a wonderful place to have social activities.

At the end of the rehabilitation project, we were offered an almost new sofa for the rooms. The sofa was in Fairlawn and clearly presented a challenge to get it to Paterson. To make it happen I asked my dad for permission to use the Abbott Brothers truck to complete this task. He readily agreed and one of the older, licensed, members agreed to drive the truck.

We picked the truck up at the mill on Totowa Avenue, drove out to Fairlawn and picked up the sofa. We started back west on Rt 4 and attempted to turn onto the intersection of Rt 4 and Rt 208. Inadvertently the truck drifted onto the recessed shoulder of the road and the truck with the sofa and four DeMolay kids turned onto its side and skidded about one hundred feet.

The good news that aside from some scrapes and bruises there were no serious injuries. The bad news was that the truck was a total loss. One of the hardest phone calls that I have ever made was the one I had to make to my dad telling him that we just destroyed his truck. In classic Stuart Abbott manner, he stayed very calm and understanding and was only concerned about the welfare of the kids that were in the truck. He neither disciplined, nor criticized me about this accident. I really was blessed with incredible parents.

The Rainbow Girls

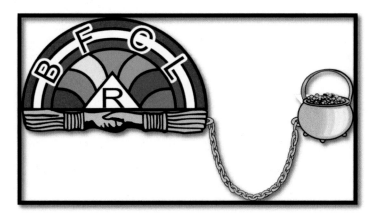

The International Order of the Rainbow for Girls (IORG) is a Masonic Youth service organization that teaches leadership training through community service. Young women learn about the value of charity and service through their work and involvement with their annual local service projects.

The order came into existence in 1922. In Paterson the Rainbow's met in the Paterson Masonic Temple on Broadway. The Rainbow Girls and the local DeMolay chapter were closely aligned, particularly in social events. Many teenage relationships and even a few marriages evolved from this close association.

In the early fifties there were often several joint activities between these two organizations. One of the most fun activities was Hayrides. These were usually done in North Haledon using a farmer's covered wagon pilled by either a horse, or a tractor. These rides were a "couples only" activity. If you were without a date for one of these events, you were in for a miserable weekend. A lot of stories, promises and passion were exchanged in the dark of those wagons.

On one of the nights when I was dateless for a hayride me and a few other single friends decide to do some mischief and play a prank on our good friend Stu Mc Kinley who of course had a date for the hayride. We found out where the riders had parked their cars and singled out Stu's car.

We jacked the car up and placed it on blocks so that the wheels were about an inch above the ground. We then hid in the background until the ride was over. Stu and his date got back in his car, fired it up and put it in gear. The wheels were spinning away, but of course the car did not move. After a few minutes of trying to figure out why the car was not moving, Stu got out and raised the hood to see if he could see anything wrong. By now the perpetrators, who are close by, are laughing hysterically. Our cover was blown, and it was time to take the car off the blocks. As I write this story I am just as amused and laughing as hard as I was on that night some 65 plus years ago. Fortunately, this prank did not harm the relationship that I have had and continue to have with Stewart McKinley. We went to elementary school together attended Paterson High Schools and Fairleigh Dickinson University together. We were fraternity brothers in DeMolay, Epsilon Nu Delta at Fairleigh, and the Masons. We are God parents to each other's children. I am blessed to have had Stu as my best friend for eighty plus years.

NEW JERSEY
GIRL FACTS

SERVING PER CONTAINER: 1 AWESOME GIRL SIGN

% Daily Value%

INTELLIGENT	90%
SARCASTIC	95%
STUBBORN	150%
REBELLIOUS	110%
PROBLEM SOLVING	100%
TELL-IT-LIKE-IT-IS	115%
LOYAL TO A FAULT	125%
LIE DETECTING	120%
SWEETEST IF TREATED WELL	200%
DANGEROUS WHEN PROVOKED	1000%

The Jersey Shore

The Spectacular Seaside Park Boardwalk

From 1944 when I was six years old, until 1955 at age 17 I was extremely fortunate to spend the month of August in Seaside Park, on the beautiful Jersey Shore.

In the early, pre–Garden State Parkway, years my folks would load up our homemade "shore trailer' with a month's worth of clothes, food and toys and we would make the three-to-four-hour trek through Little Falls, Cedar Grove, South Mountain Reservation, Millburn., and Edison where we would finally reach the Edison Bridge over the Raritan River. From there it was a straight shot onto Route 9 and towards Toms River and Seaside Heights. It was not a very comfortable trip with four to five kids and our parents jammed into one car.

Don, Doug & George Abbott - Late 40's @ 45 Emerson Ave -Paterson with the "Shore Trailer" made by our Dad from "Jim Dandy" Trailer Plans

For most of the summers we always had either adjoining, or nearby houses with our close family friends the Millerchip's from Paterson and the Methvin's from Closter, NJ.

By the early 60's the Millerchip's and Methvin's had purchased adjoining homes on Brynmar Avenue in North Lavallette. My parents then moved permanently to a Bay front home on Haddonfield Avenue also in North Lavalette

All three families were real beach addicts and as long as it wasn't raining, we would typically spend six to eight hours on the beautiful Seaside Park Beaches every day. It is a miracle that we all did not have serious skin cancer issues later in life. At the time we had no idea that thiseven was an issue.

The boys in the families would often skip the beach day and go crabbing and snapper blue fishing on the Fifth Avenue Pier in Seaside Park. We would almost always come home with a bushel basket of New Jersey's best blue claws.

The evenings were another busy time for the kids. At least several nights each week we would walk a mile plus on the Boardwalk into the Amusement area in Seaside Heights. There we would go on as many of the rides as our budget would allow, always have some French Fries with vinegar at JoJo's, a Kohrs Frozen Custard cone and occasionally either a Taylor Ham Sandwich, or Pizza slice at Maruca's.

Like all young teenagers we never had enough money. To supplement our meager funds Tommy Millerchip and I would often find an open area on the Seaside Heights Boardwalk where we could access the area below the most aggressive rides Those that tended to cause change to fall out of the rider's pockets and then fall though the Boardwalk cracks were our target areas to search. This enterprising activity usually generated $2.00 to $4.00 of found money that was immediately put back in circulation on the next night's outing.

Rainy days at the shore were a real bummer and a real headache for our mothers. To break up the boredom the boys would walk to the B & B Five & Ten store in Seaside Park and buy a model airplane kit. That was usually good for at least a day, or two of entertainment.

During one multiple day rain event the tension between siblings got to the critical point. I started to chase my brother Don around the house when he ran onto the glassed-in front porch. Unfortunately, he did not stop before breaking one of the windows with his shoulder. To this day he still has a scar on his back from that fracas.

The Casino Pier Pre-Hurricane Sandy

Most of the pier was in the Ocean after the Hurricane. The Roller Coaster Ride on the right-hand corner was on the national news for days after.

Newark – Country Music & Burlesque

Country Music:

While growing up in Paterson in the early 1950's,I would rush to get away from school to catch the last hour of a country music radio show called the "Hometown Frolic" on Newark station WAAT.

In the 1950's, as a kid growing up with three brothers and one sister in Paterson,I discovered WAAT, Don Larkin and the Hometown Frolic and fell in love with country music.

Don Larkin

    I was a child of perhaps 10 or 11 when I joined the thousands of country music fans in New York, New Jersey, eastern Pennsylvania, and Connecticut, who listened to Don

Larkin on his Hometown Frolic show on station WAAT from Newark. It was on Don's show that I first heard the driving rhythms and harmonies of Bill Monroe's bluegrass music and the plaintive songs of Hank Williams and other country artists of that day. "Larkin Barkin" began each show with Gene Autry's "Back in the Saddle Again" and ended with the same artist's "Goodbye Little Darlin" .

The Hometown Frolic opened a whole new world for me – the country music of Hank Williams, Ernest Tubb, Grandpa Jones, Hank Snow, Webb Pierce, Faron Young and so many others, and the bluegrass music of Monroe, Johnny and Jack, Flatt & Scruggs, the Louvin Brothers, Reno &Smiley and the Stanley Brothers.

Don Larkin and Marty Robbins

I owe my appreciation of country music to the Hometown Frolic and its fabled deejay, Don Larkin, who ran the show for 11 years, from 1950 when he took it over to 1961 when WAAT was sold, changed its call letters and cancelled the Hometown Frolic.

Don Larkin and Patsy Cline

While spinning Country Music records for his radio audience, Don Larkin also became a concert promotor in the New York metropolitan area bringing live Country Music concerts for the first time to audiences in this part of the country. Don brought artists such as Bill Monroe, Faron Young, Webb Pierce, Marty Robbins, Patsy Cline Elton Britt, and Johnny Cash.

In Newark these concerts were usually held at the Terrace Ballroom. The "Clan" from Cliff's was always well represented at these shows.

Earlier in his radio career, young Don. Larkin, who played piano quite well, was prevailed upon to accompany a skinny young singer from nearby Hoboken making his radio audition. The name of the kid making his radio debut? Frank Sinatra. Don then left radio for a while to earn his law degree but before he could use it, he joined the military to make his contribution to vanquishing the Nazis by serving as a spotter pilot in the European theater during WWII.

Burlesque

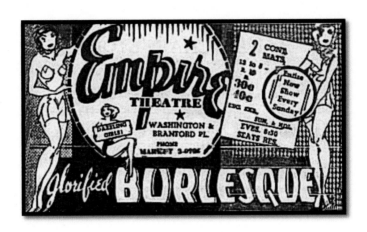

In the mid-fifties I was palling around with a couple of guys who were older than me and who already had their driver's license. After we learned about the Newark Burlesque Shows it was only a matter of time before we made the trip to Newark to see what they were all about. Getting into the theater was a challenge as the minimum age was eighteen. At the time I had a very dark and heavy beard and that probably helped get past the ticket takers. At this point in the fifties these shows were by far the most risqué form of entertainment available. These shows were an incredible eye-opening experience for a sheltered and naive teenager. We never discussed our attendance with even close friends. However, by 2023 behavior standards it was no big deal.

The Empire Burlesque Theatre enjoyed a unique place among Newark's downtown theatres in the first half of the 20th century. It filled a gap in Downtown Newark stage and screen presentations unmatched by any other area theatre.

The Empire Theatre opened in 1912 at 265 Washington Street, at the corner of Branford Place, just one block in from Market Street.

It was a place, where for a very modest admission payment, a man could get his fill of girls, gags, and music, in that order.

Early admission prices, according to an old Empire play bill were as low as 30 cents.

The chief attraction, of course, was the girls -- both the strippers and dancing chorus line which showed as much of their bodies as the law permitted.

The gags were performed by comic teams and included tried and true time-honored skits, and sometimes take-offs on recent Broadway shows.

The music, played by a pit orchestra, aside from the bumps and grinds for the strippers, was the popular music of the day intermingled with old-time favorites and ballads.

The 'Burlesque' and It's Patrons

A Newark movie owner of the 1930s and 1940s, friendly with the Empire management, recalled recently that the Empire was a beautiful theatre of about 1,000 seats and with a long balcony that brought upstairs patrons down close to the stage, and sat directly over the higher-paying customers in the downstairs orchestra seats.

He also recalled that in the era when the Burlesque Theatre in Newark was in its heyday, many middle-aged patrons, especially church-goers, while burlesque habitués, considered going to the Empire to view the unclad bosoms as something sinful, and before going in to buy their ticket, would look both ways to ensure that no friends, neighbors, or fellow church parishioners were in sight before buying their ticket.

Inside the Theatre, he said, they would usually sit way back from the stage so as not to be too visible to others who were also there for the same reason and might recognize them.

The Comics

As in every standard Empire show, there were always comics, usually a pair, a 'top banana' accompanied by a sidekick or straight man.

Their comedy involved sexual innuendo, but the focus was on making fun of what people go through in pursuit of it.

Usually it was two men, but sometimes there would be a man-woman duo which might involve a conversation filled with ambiguities: The woman might say something innocent, and the man would think she meant something else.

If two men were involved, there would also be a lot of talk leaning toward the vulgar, but something that would get big laughs.

The Strippers

Although the Empire in Newark opened in 1913 as a variety show house, the strip tease was not added to burlesque until the 1920s when vaudeville began feeling the competition from motion pictures and added the strip tease as a vehicle for attracting men away from the movies.

The name strippers of the 1930s and 1940s that played the Empire included Margie Hart, Lili St. Cyr in her bath routine,

Rosita Royce with her trained doves covering her partial nudity, and the fiery red-headed sensation, Georgia Sothern who made the biggest impression on this young pre-World War II burlesque attendee.1

The Empire enjoyed an unexpected surge of business in the late 1930s after New York City Mayor, Fiorella LaGuardia, shut down the striptease shows that were mostly along 42nd Street, and drove the patrons of the strippers across the Hudson River to the Empire in Newark, and the Hudson Theatre in Union City.

Ann Corio who starred as a burlesque queen and rose to greatness as a star of stage and as a bestseller book author was quoted in her March 1999 obituary in the New York Times as saying this of her life as a stripper: "We were naughty and bawdy, but never vulgar."

End of Burlesque in Newark

By the 1950s, TV and other forms of entertainment reduced attendance. Simultaneously, anti-burlesque amendments were added to the city's theatre ordinances making it virtually impossible to continue operations.

With the arrest of 21 burlesque performers in the preceding two weeks, and a license revocation threatened by the city, the Empire management finally closed its doors forever on February 14, 1957.

In July 1958, the Empire Theatre building was torn down and the land on which it stood was leveled and paved over to become a parking lot for downtown Newark shoppers.

Television in The 40's & 50's

For the people born in the late thirties and early forties significant evolutionary change has been a constant in their lives that continues unabated to the present day.

I was born in 1938. In my lifetime I have personally experienced the consequences of the following inventions and technological improvements. The list is a personal one and is not meant to be an accurate portrayal of a carefully researched summary.

❖ Television –The earliest, although limited functionality televisions appeared in the 1920's when an inventor named Charles Jenkins was awarded over 400 patents for his work. It took another 40 years for the technology to gain enough refinement for commercial success. Those with television sets in the late forties quickly found that their life was quickly and permanently altered.

❖ Antibiotics – Development was accelerated by WWII.

❖ Air Conditioning – First experience was in movie theaters, followed by millions of window units and finally Central Air Conditioning. Later followed by Air Conditioning for cars.

- ❖ Transistor radios
- ❖ Jet engines –I was an Aircraft Engines major at Paterson Tech 1952-1956. There were no jet engines in our shop. The Korean War in 1950-1953 was the first combat use of jet aircraft. I flew on my first jet flight in 1959 on a flight from Los Angeles to Newark. Under six hours coast to coast on a TWA Boeing 707, incredible! The jet engine revolutionized air travel with quantum improvements in safety, flight time, and economics. After 40 years of business travel on jet aircraft I have accumulated over 1,000,000 miles without an incident.
- ❖ Fax Machines for business communications. This was big time development in my early business career.
- ❖ Xerox/Copy Machines meant no more carbon paper and obsoleted the mimeograph machine.
- ❖ Video Recorders
- ❖ The IBM Selectric Typewriter. Made all other typewriters obsolete.
- ❖ CDs for Music, Movies and Data
- ❖ Satellites for navigation, communication, and entertainment

- ❖ Personal Computers. They really gained a footing in the late 80's and 90's. The improvements just keep on comingi.e. The iPad etc.
- ❖ Cell Phones – A blessing and a curse.

Television

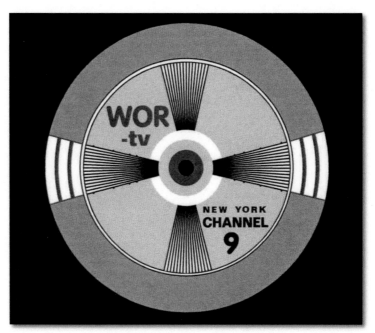

Test Pattern from The Forties

The changes brought through inventions, as well as those created by technological refinements, have been constant and life changing. In this chapter we will review some of the major developments with Television that really came on the scene in the post war years of 1946 through the mid-fifties.

In 1948 my family was blessed with having the second TV set on Emerson Ave. The set was a twelve-inch Transvision brand product. The Transvision sets were not sold in ready to use form. They were kits that the buyer had to solder and mount hundreds of capacitors, resistors, transformers, and tubes on the aluminum chassis. The picture tube was a monster that had to be close to 24" long.

My dad and our family doctor, Dr Edwin Allen, each bought one of these kits and spent the next three plus months assembling them. When finished, they worked, but not well. After a trip to the Dealer's shop there was a vast improvement in the picture quality. We used this basic TV set for several years before replacing it with a larger screen set.

Our basement recreation room quickly became a very popular place for not only my family, but also our extended family of relatives that also lived on Emerson Avenue. Must see shows included The Texaco Star Theater with Milton Berle, The Toast of The Town with Ed Sullivan and special events such as the Ringling Brothers Circus, and Boxing Matches.

An Early Transvision TV

A completed Transvision Kit Ready for The Cabinet

~ 137 ~

ARE <u>YOU</u> READY FOR TELEVISION?

The time is here for America to revise its concepts of its living-rooms, its classrooms, its town halls. The time is here to become familiar with new measurements of human progress...economic, political, scientific.

For full-scale Television is near...a force of unparalleled power. Television will carry new thoughts, new hopes, new products into millions of homes. It will stir men's minds and hearts in a matter of moments. We will watch the truly wonderful tomorrow take shape before our eyes.

DuMont will provide you with the finest in Television reception...sight and sound. DuMont quality will be assured by impressive prewar pioneering in Television, by vigorous wartime development, by highly specialized production "know how," by advantageous patents.

Indeed, the world stands on the threshold of an astonishing age...DuMont Television is ready...Are *You*?

Copyright 1944, Allen B. DuMont Laboratories, Inc.

DuMONT *Precision Electronics and Television*

ALLEN B. DuMONT LABORATORIES, INC., GENERAL OFFICES AND PLANT, 2 MAIN AVENUE, PASSAIC, N. J.
TELEVISION STUDIOS AND STATION WABD, 515 MADISON AVENUE, NEW YORK 22, NEW YORK

New Yorker - Nov. 25. 1944

Engineer Allen B. DuMont (1901-1965) was a New Jersey resident and one of the true pioneers of television technology in the 1930s. The sets manufactured by his company, DuMont Laboratories, in Passaic, New Jersey, were considered among the finest in the industry. The problem was nobody was buying the darned things. TV sets were very expensive—about $5,000 in today's money.

The company was founded in 1931, in an Upper Montclair garage, by inventor Allen B. DuMont, with its headquarters in nearby Clifton. Among the company's developments were durable cathode ray tubes (CRTs) that would be used for TV. Prior to this development the very short life, typically one day, of the tubes prevented serious commercialization of Television sets. The new

CRTs produced by DuMont had a service life of 1,000 + hours. Consumer television sets became viable beginning in 1938.

One of the major, fundamental problems of the TV Broadcasting industry was the lack of any regularly scheduled broadcasts at that time. Undaunted and despite not having any kind of show-business background, the engineer decided to produce his very own television broadcasts, including game shows, dramas, comedies, and sports. This led to the mid-August 1946 debut of the upstart DuMont Network, the first television network to challenge the supremacy of CBS and NBC.

DuMont's parent company was a pioneer in early television technology, but largely because it lacked the support of a radio network, the DuMont Television Network struggled to compete with the emerging television networks created by the radio powerhouses of CBS and NBC.

Moreover, between 1946 and 1956 did broadcast some 200-television series. Some were groundbreaking concepts. Shows such as Life is worth Living by Bishop Fulton J Sheen, Captain Video & His Video Rangers, and Cavalcade of Stars (1949-1952) on which Jackie Gleason introduced the sketches that evolved into the Honeymooners series on CBS.

Lacking the financial clout of NBC and CBS, the DuMont Network was in decline by the end of the forties. The merger of

ABC with Paramount Theaters pushed DuMont into fourth place in the Nielsen ratings. This fact with severe restriction on network expansion by the FCC were devasting blows. In 1955 Paramount, who was a part owner of DuMont seized control of the network. The last Program aired by DuMont was Boxing from St, Nicholas Arena in 1956.

Acknowledgements

There are many outstanding photos dispersed throughout this book. Many of them were extracted from numerous Facebook postings on various Paterson Pages. To the best of my knowledge, they are all in the Public Domain. However, I would be negligent not to recognize several contributions that have enriched my knowledge of Paterson's history.

For years I have enjoyed many posts by Patty Henderson on her Paterson NJ Facebook site. I know of no other person who so enthusiastically captures and shares her views and knowledge of the city I was born and raised in. From the bottom of my heart, thank you Patty for not only enriching this book, but also giving me the inspiration to write it.

Another dedicated Paterson cheerleader is Bernard Jaz Payne. His eye for the historical sites, as well as human interest stories is a treasure for all fans of Paterson memorabilia.

A very special thank you is in order for my dear friend Kathleen Marshall Kazanjian who provided the initial encouragement to tackle this project and then continually offered proofreading and a lot of constructive comments along the way. I could not have done this without you, my sweet lady!

Last, but not least, a very special thanks to all of the un-named Facebook Paterson followers whose commentaries and photos were so valuable in developing all of the Paterson historical dialog in this book.